Seasons on Lookout Mountain

Michèle Vachon Beaudin

Mentone, Alabama, USA

Book design by Michèle V. Beaudin

www.immigesandwords.com
www.immiges.com

michele@immiges.com

ISBN 978-0-615-32453-1

Library of Congress Control Number: 2009909892

Printed in the United States of America

First Edition

Seasons on Lookout Mountain

Let me take you into my world
where water roars in the spring,
flows gently in the summer,
pauses to reflect the beauty of fall
and cools its shores in the winter.

This is a voyage of beauty and serenity
in a world we can still fall in love with.

Sunrises, sunsets, all serve to make us yearn
for a simpler life.

If you chance upon this wonder of the south,
learn to keep it in tune with its natural evolution.
Only take back its peace to share and sweet memories to cherish.

To all the wonderful people of Lookout Mountain,
this is my gift of thanks for having kept this natural treasure
one of the most beautiful and pristine natural wonders
that can still be found in this slice of America.

(The cover photographic composition, "Unglued" is from an original photo of a woman contemplating the depth of the Little River Canyon)

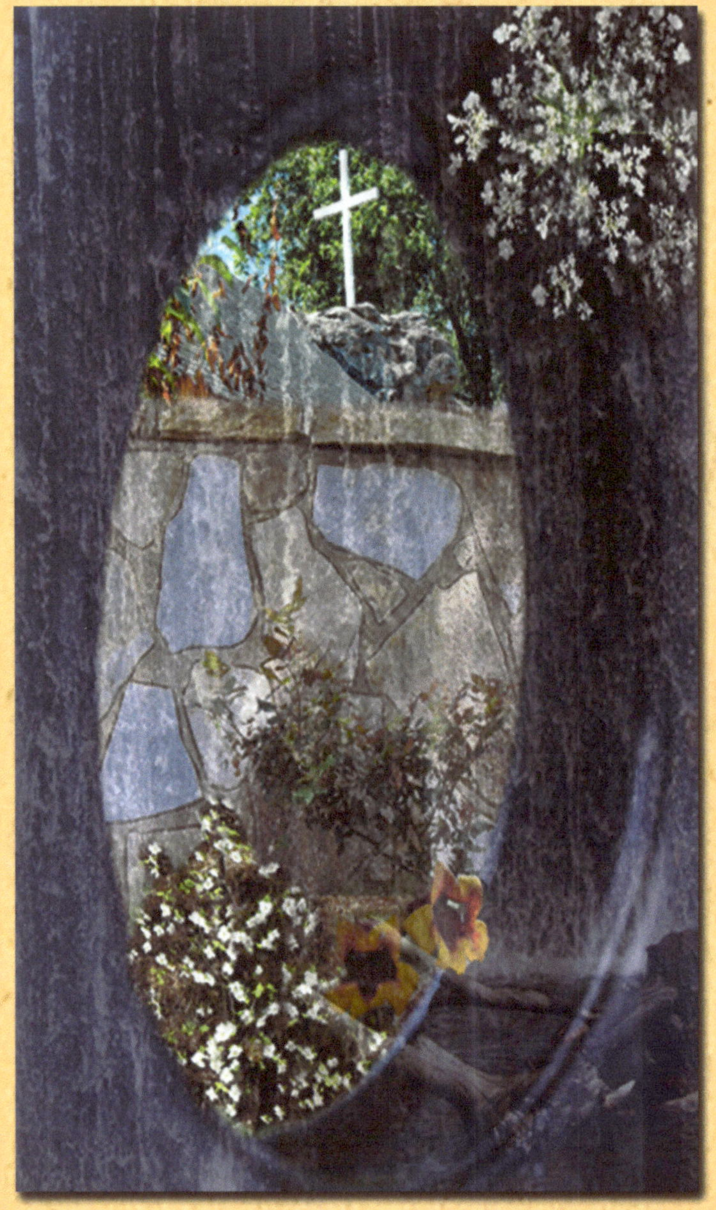

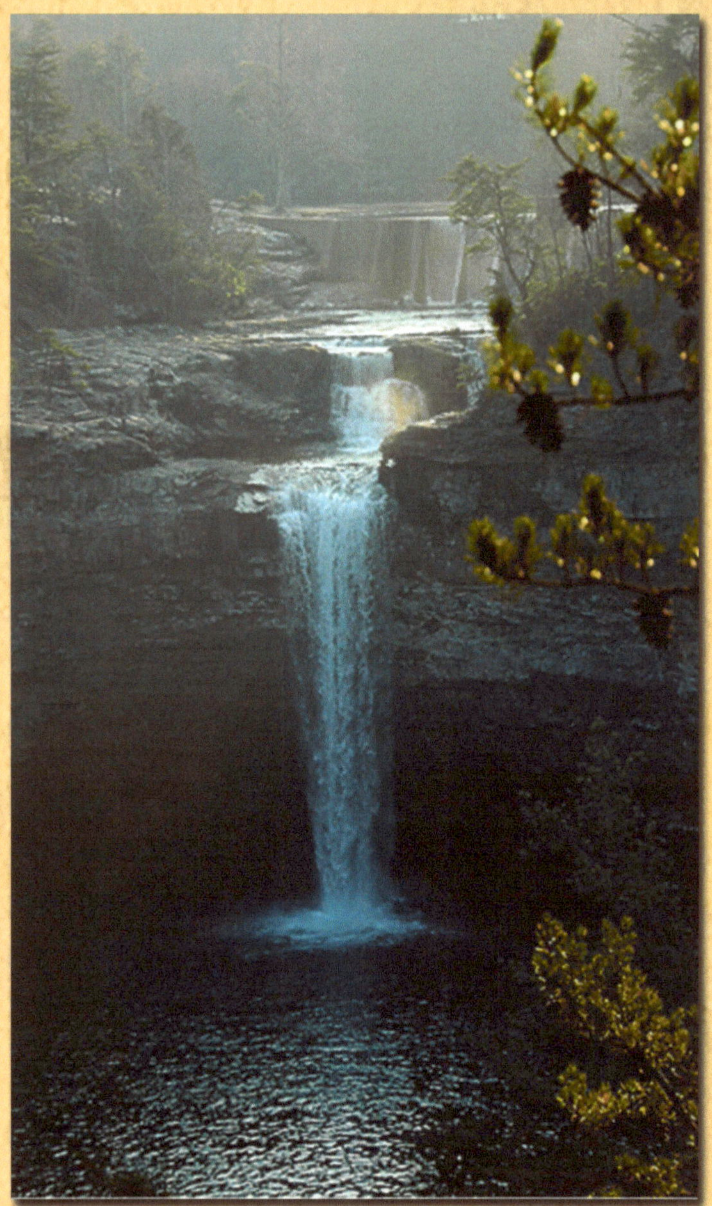

“Day Dreaming near the Lake”

Spring has arrived and the dance of Seasons begins.

One old tire hangs from a tree, filled with the daydreams of a little
girl who longs for carefree times to come.
She dreams of vacations, dreams of flowers, dreams of love,
her dreams all begging for attention in her mind’s eye,
all waiting to come true.

A long trek at dawn in the wilderness and the DeSoto falls appear in
all their majesty. The trail will soon be covered by new growth and
become impassable… but there is still time.

Walking the trail, all you see is a rough, rock-filled path
framed by tall trees and unruly shrubs.
Then, the branches spread out.
The path ends.

Valleys appear at your feet and mountains emerge on the horizon.
Hanging from a cliff, you can now see a trickle of river below,
all that is left to flow from the lake fed by the falls.

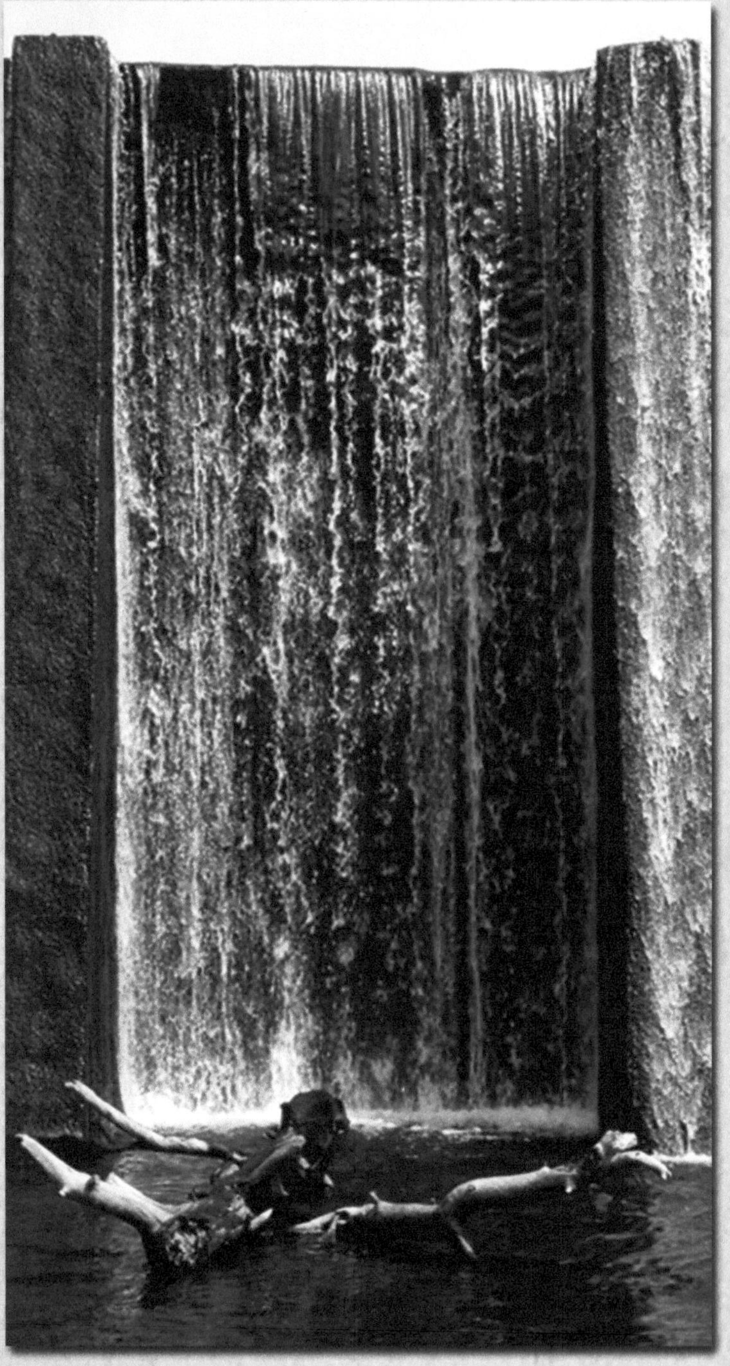

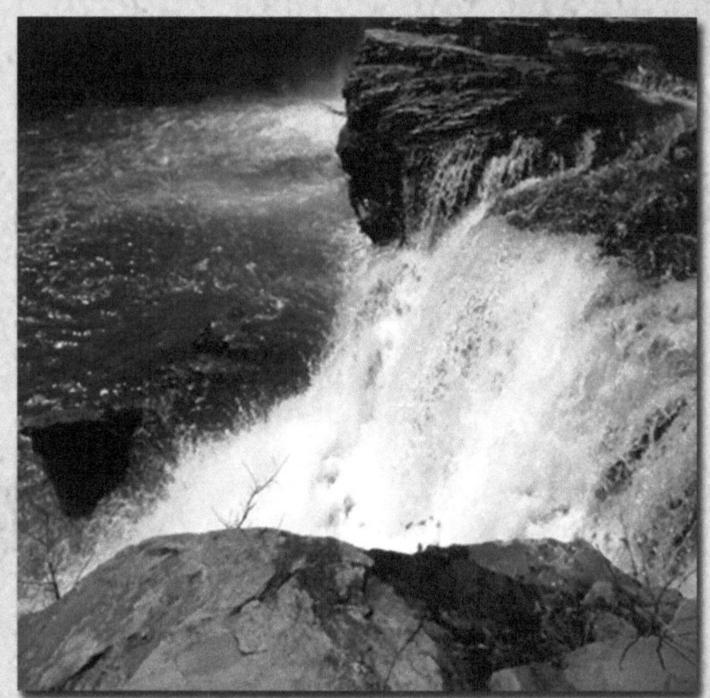

"Water"

Always a source of inspiration, water sparkles like so many diamonds and carves its way through rocks as it starts its long journey.

Never beginning, never ending only travelling incessantly towards the sea, giving life along the way.

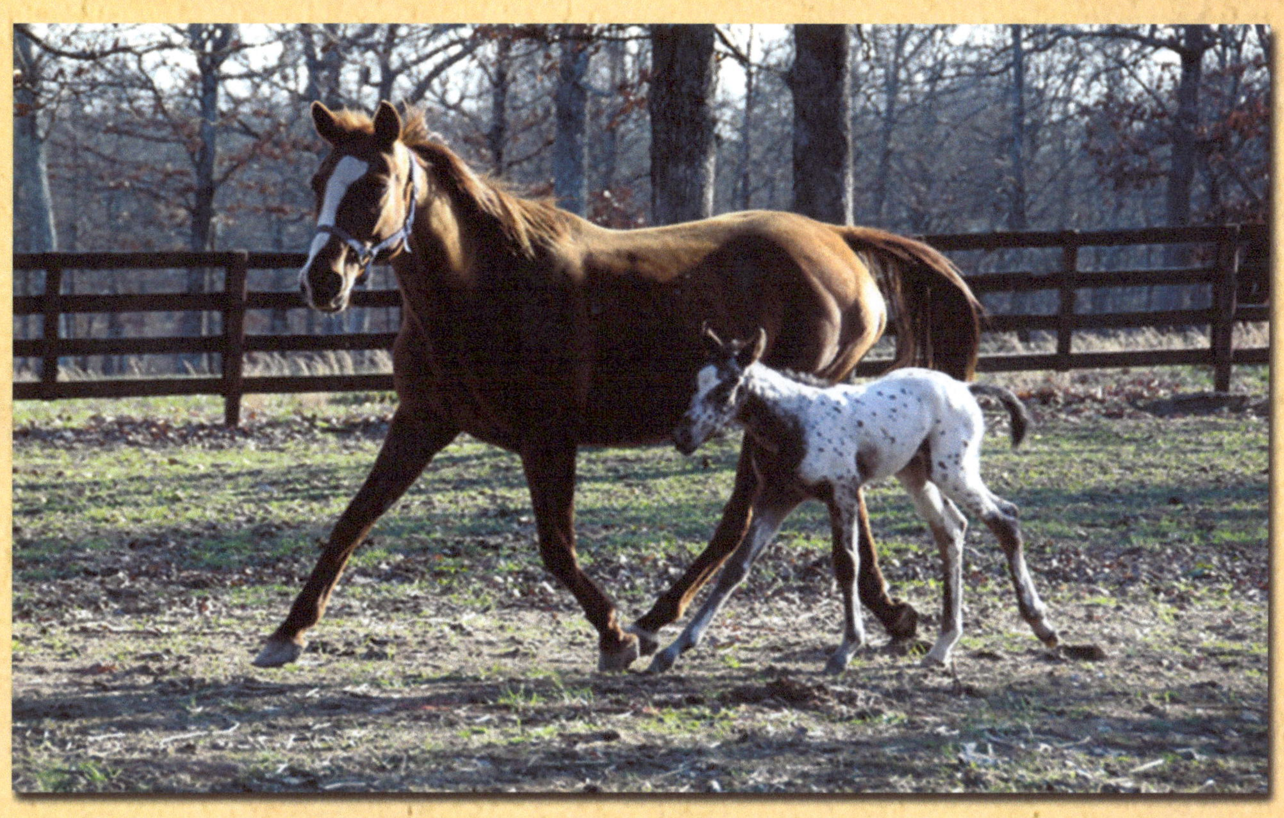

“A New Life”

Born yesterday, the foal
learns how to experience life on the mountain range.
from his proud mother.

Another miracle of nature to behold.

"Morning has Broken"

The smoke is rising… or falling.
Sunrise has come and gone.
Only the miracle of a perfect morning remains.
Let the sun freeze in its tracks so we can meditate longer.

From a morning of prayer where a rock grows into the
sanctuary or in a chapel meant for lovers.
To a day filled with sites and sounds of waterfalls and
children playing in fields of green,.
To an evening which will take you to the brink of the
mountain to spy on other states, all looking up to where you
stand, waiting for the moon to rise.

Let the moment lull you to a sense of peace and contentment
that can only be achieved when communing with nature.

Tomorrow will bring more joy if you open up your soul to
the wonders of life.

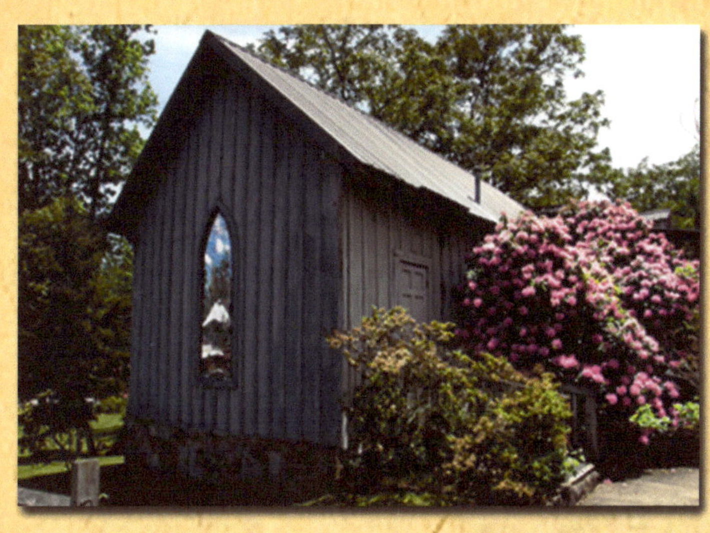

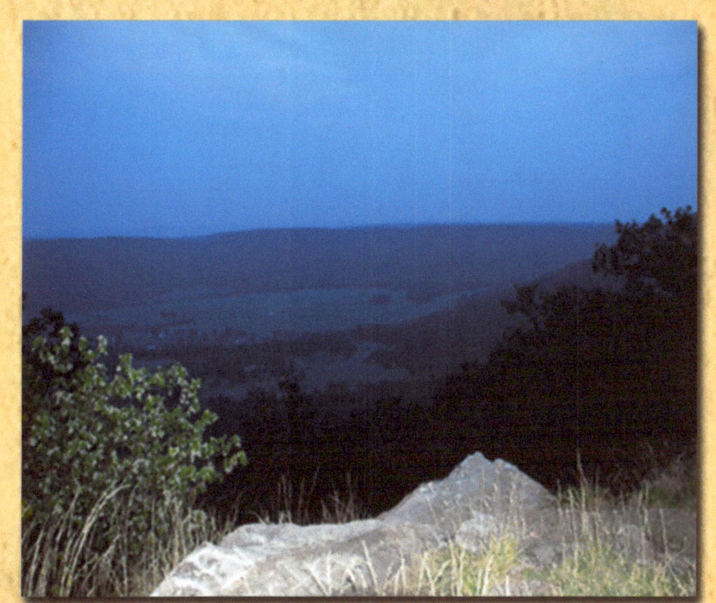

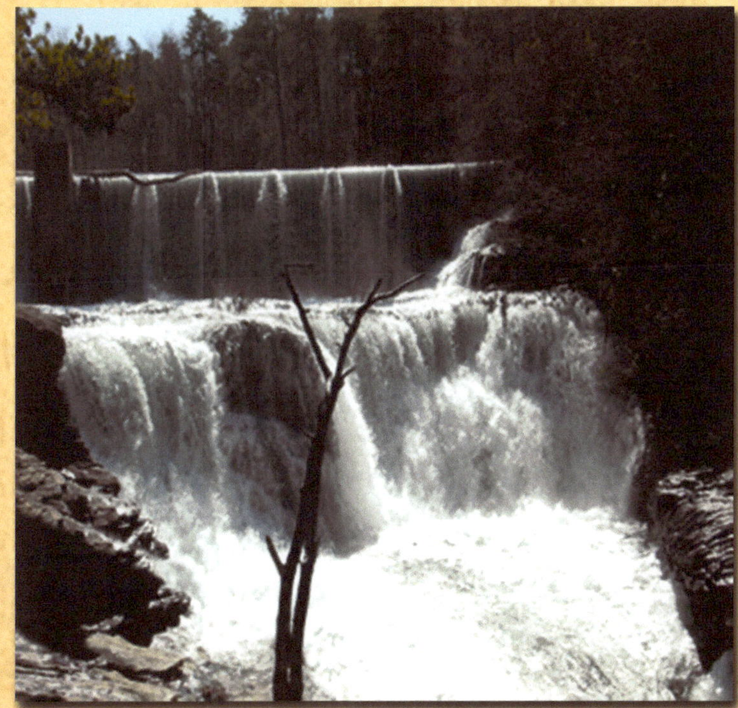

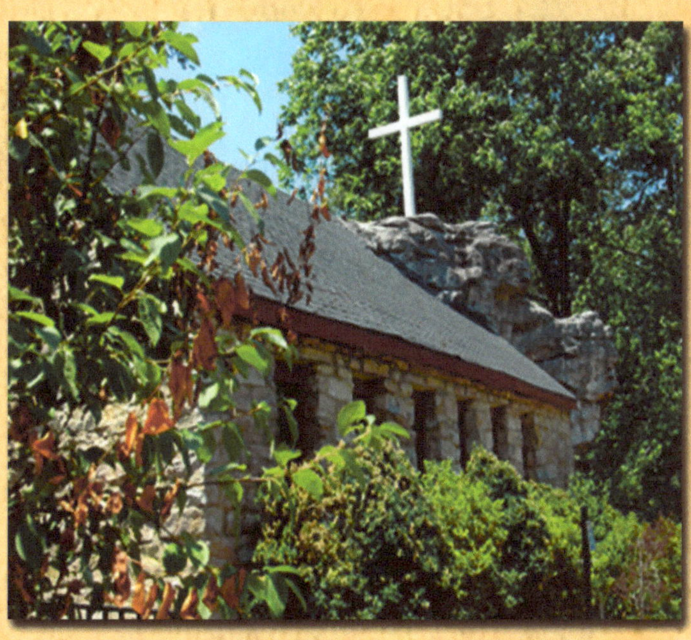

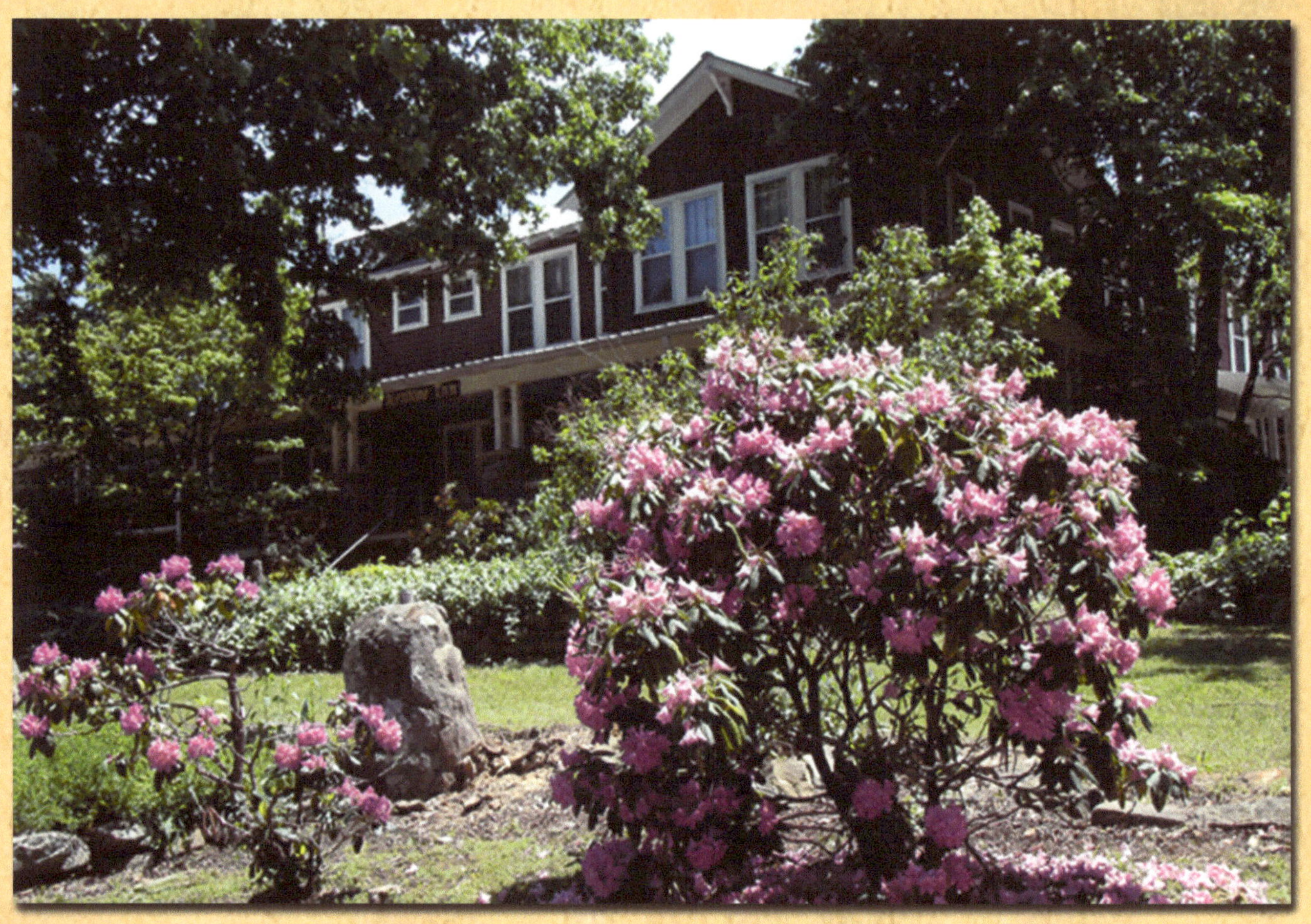

“Rhododendrons, Azaleas, Wild Flowers”

Shrubs in bloom are signs of hope for the summer to be bountiful.

Their fresh scents and colors will energize your life and feed your soul.

Flowers remind you to laugh, love, sing and to always keep your dreams alive.

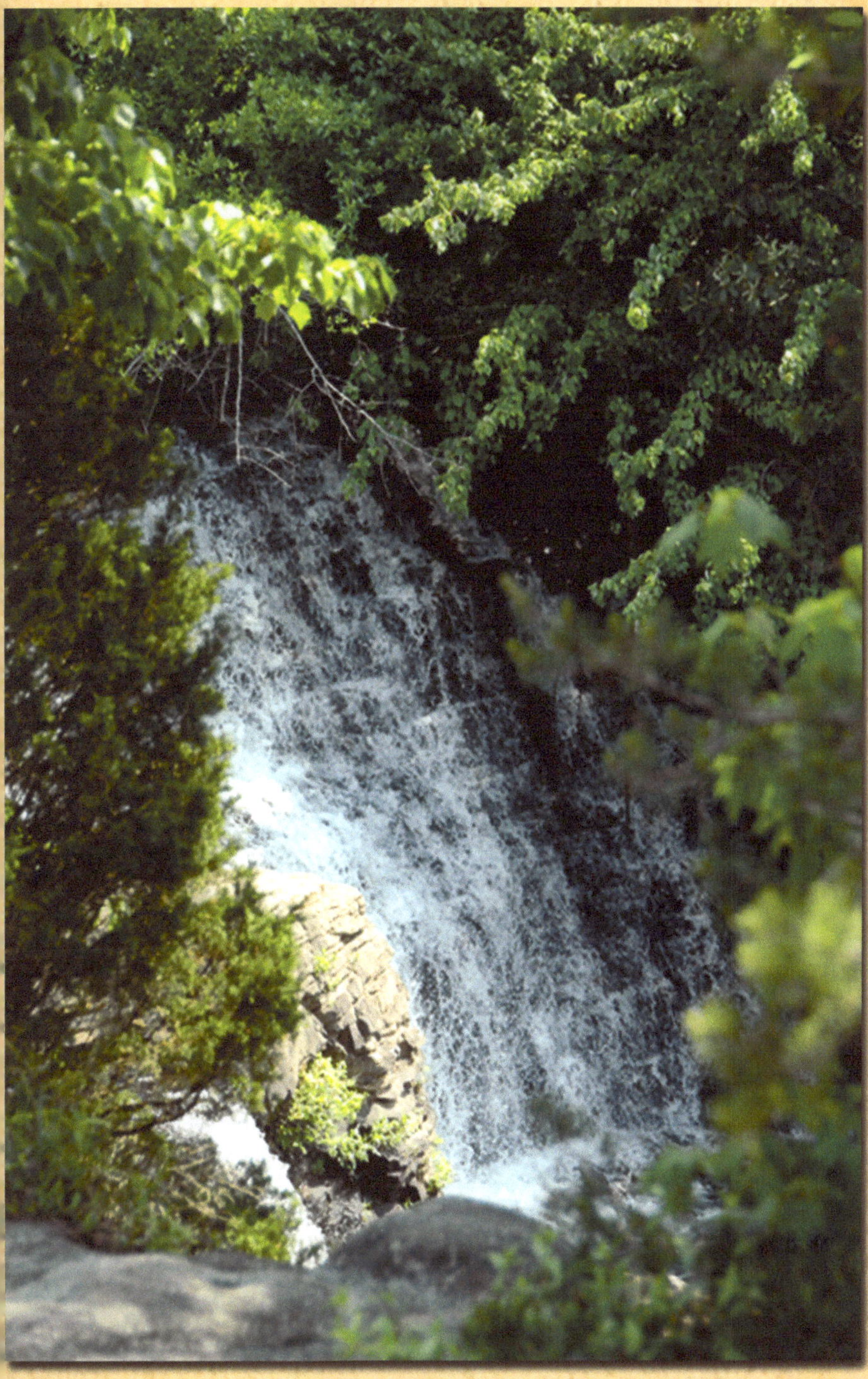

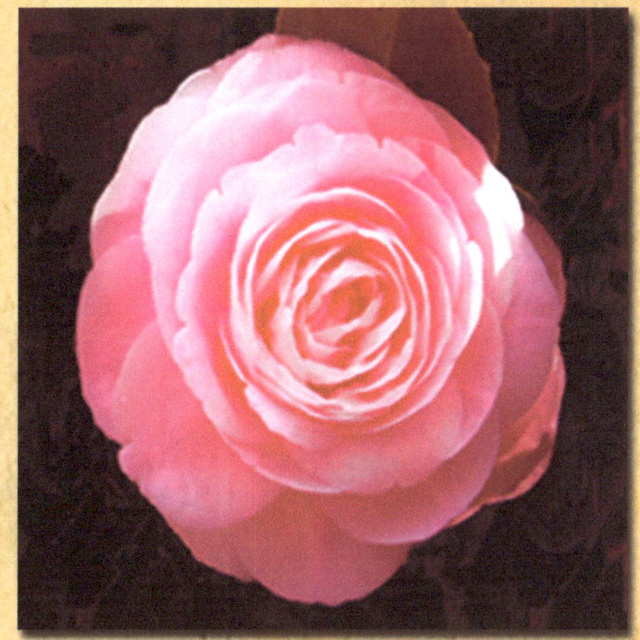

“Always More Flowers”

Blooms of all colors surround you as you make your way on the mountain.

Everywhere you look, Day Lillies, Camelias, Rhododendrons, all growing wild, the perfect accessories to complement the nature trails that crisscross Lookout Mountain.

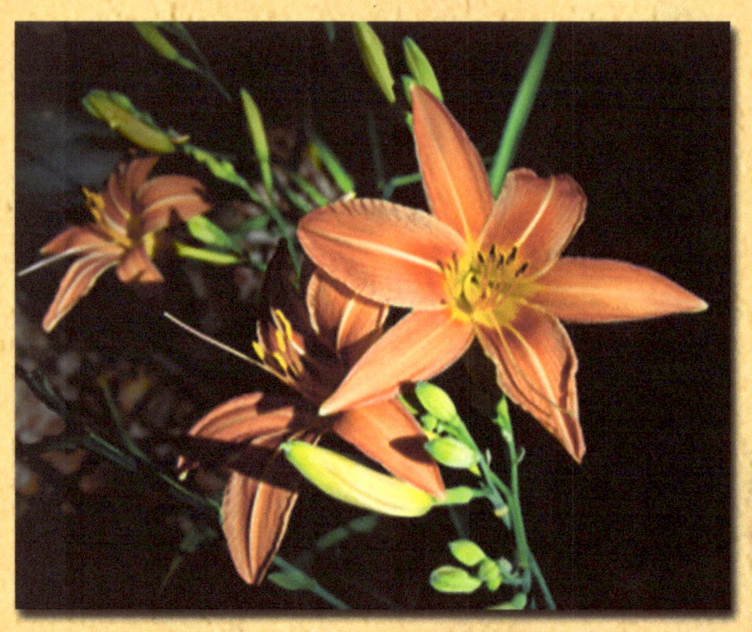

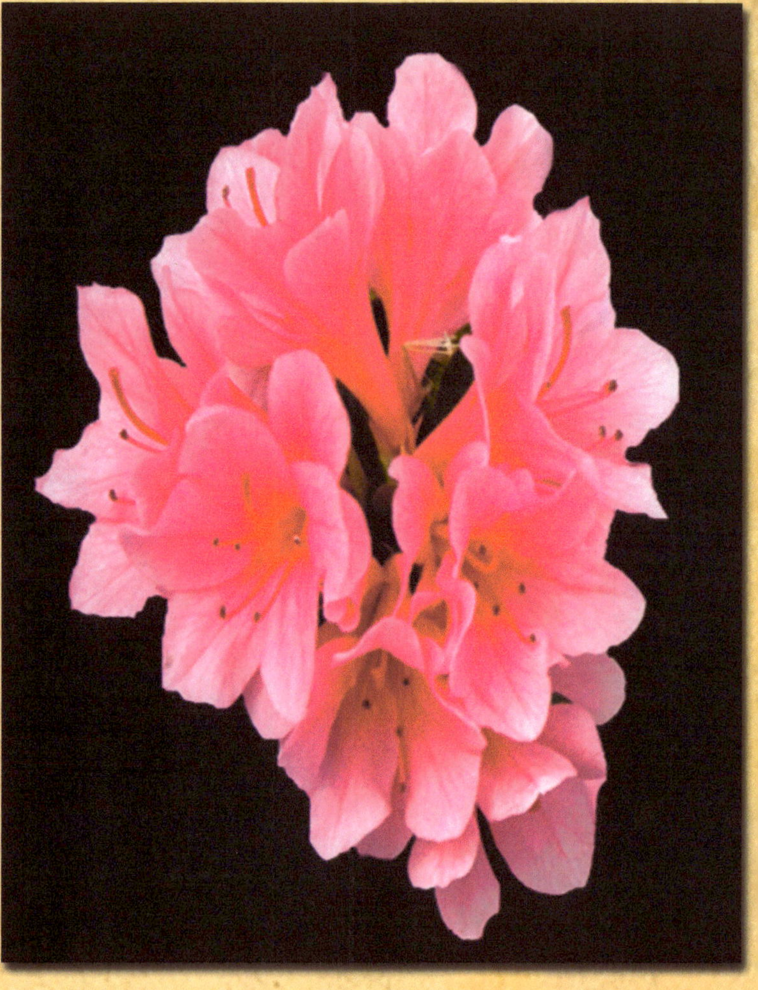

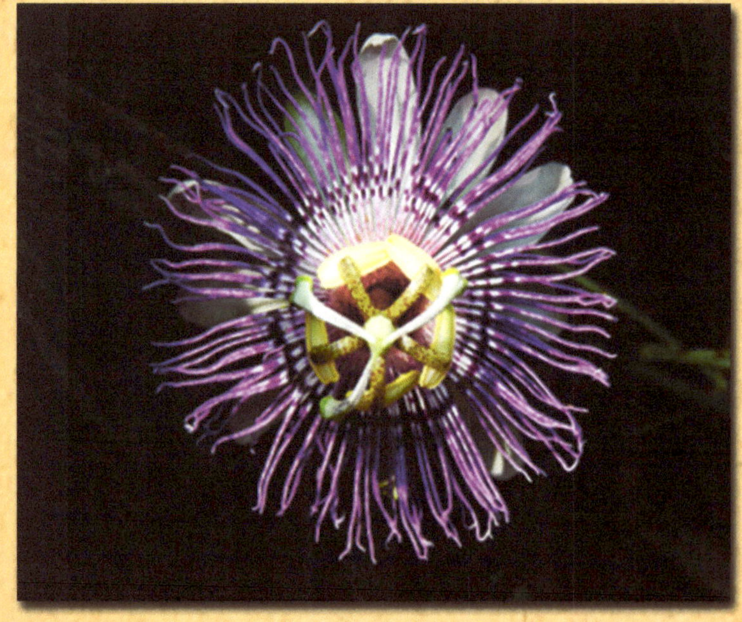

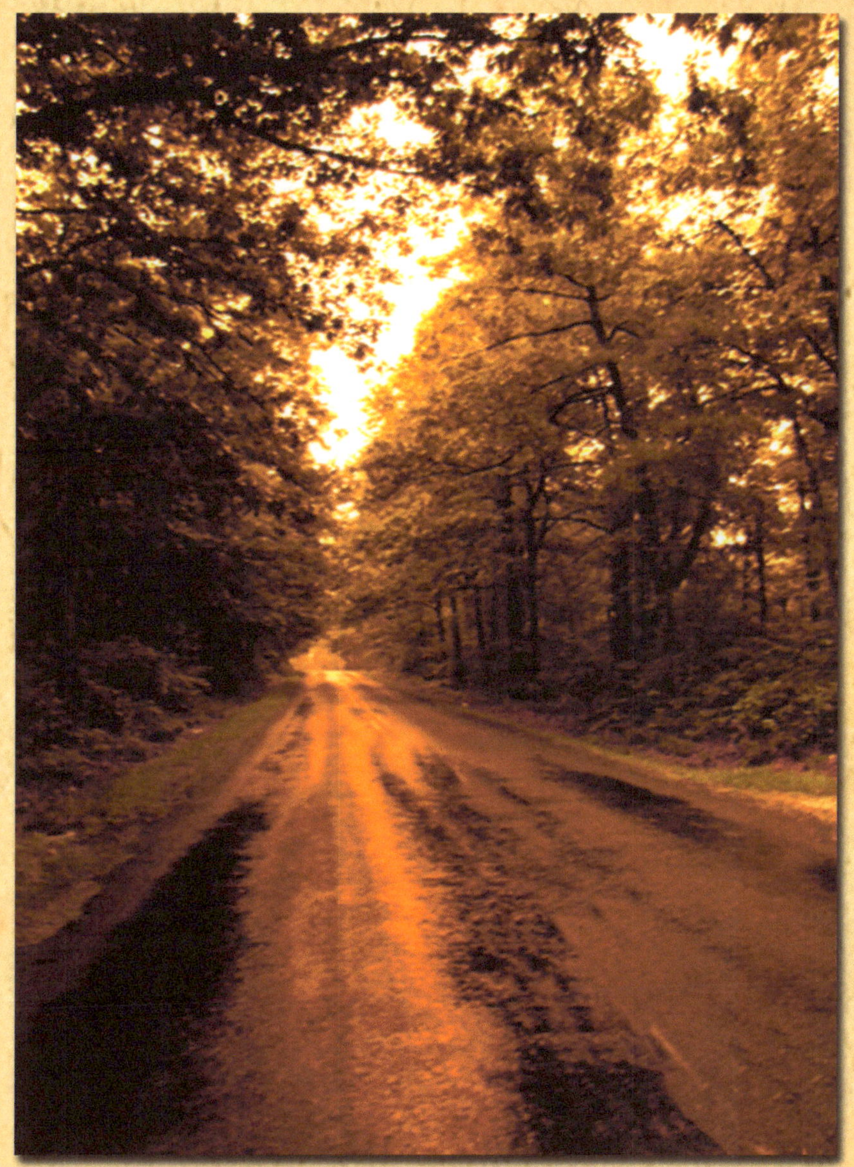

"Stormy Sky"

Late one summer, the sun quietly settled,
unaware of the storm brewing across the sky.

A yellow cocoon shrouded the lane,
then paled, revealing a vanilla sky.

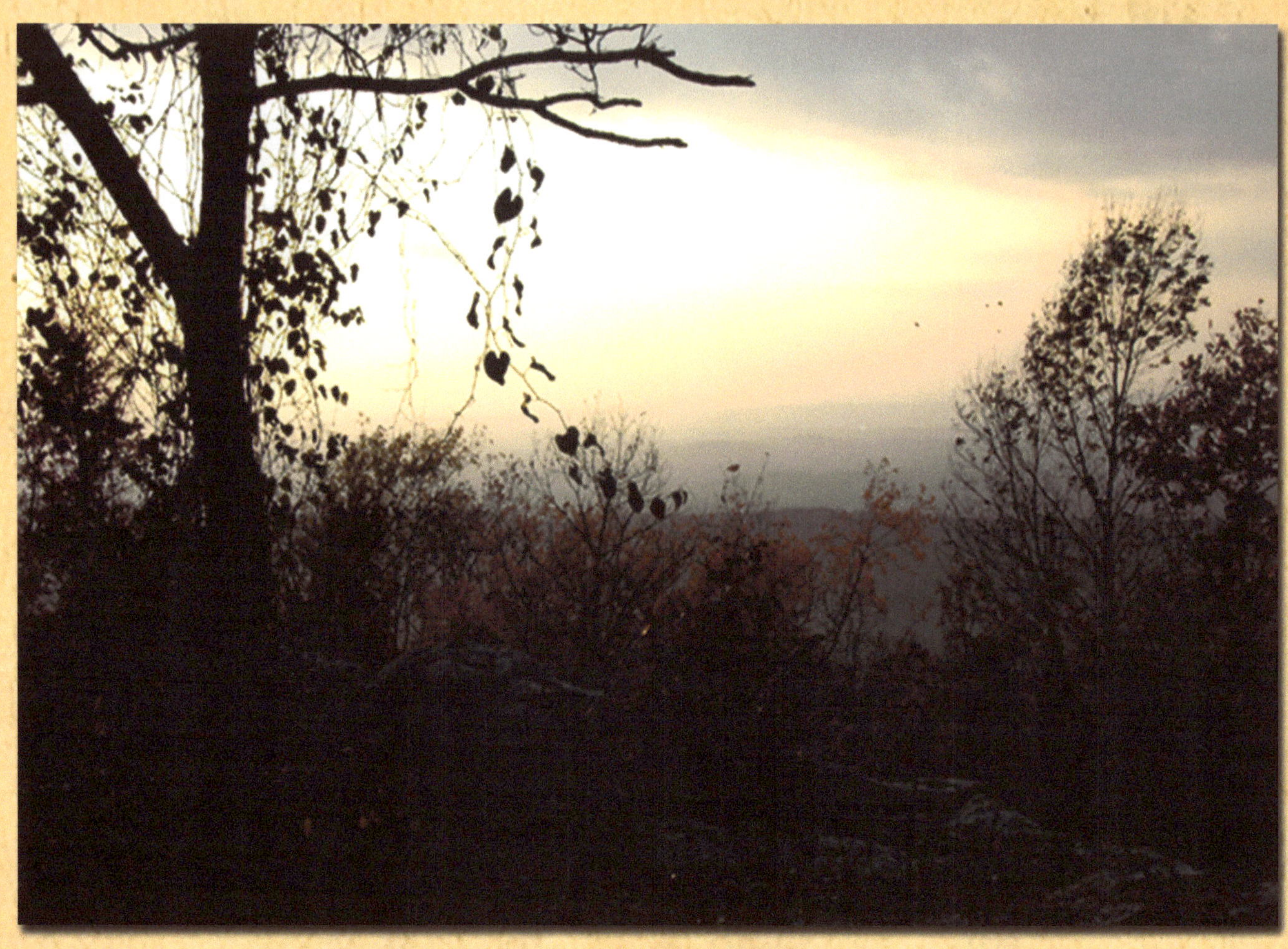

“Fall Sunset”

Not yet cold, no longer warm,
the mountain invites you to stop at its brow
to feel the winter air which will rise from the valley
once the sun sets on the horizon.

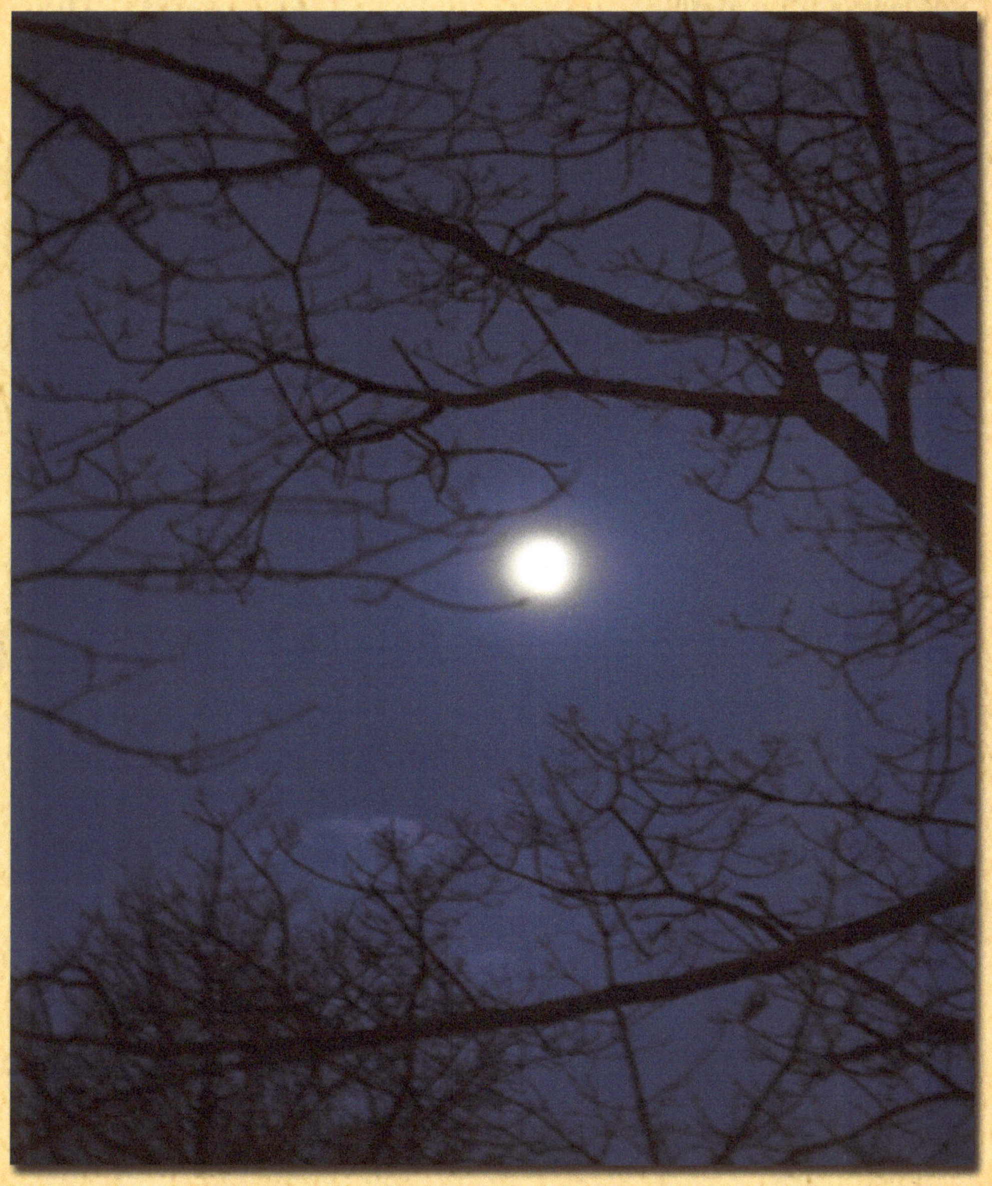

“Moon over Mentone”

Once in a blue moon, often at harvest time, a cool night will keep music flowing on the mountain until dawn.

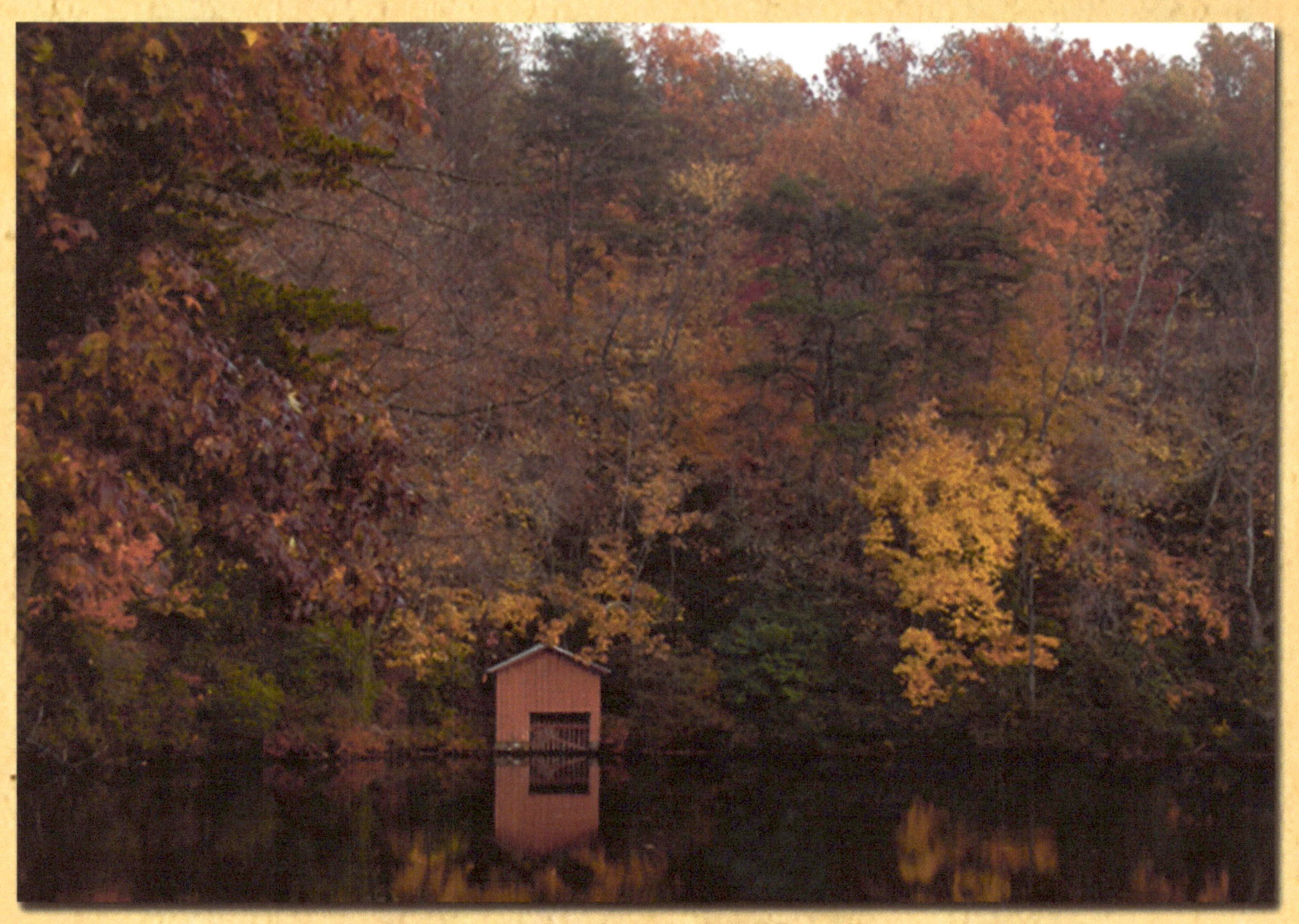

“A time for Reflection”

No one cares about the rain, automn has
come, we know the sky will soon clear.

We have to capture the essence of nature in
its crescendo of color just before it falls
asleep for the winter.

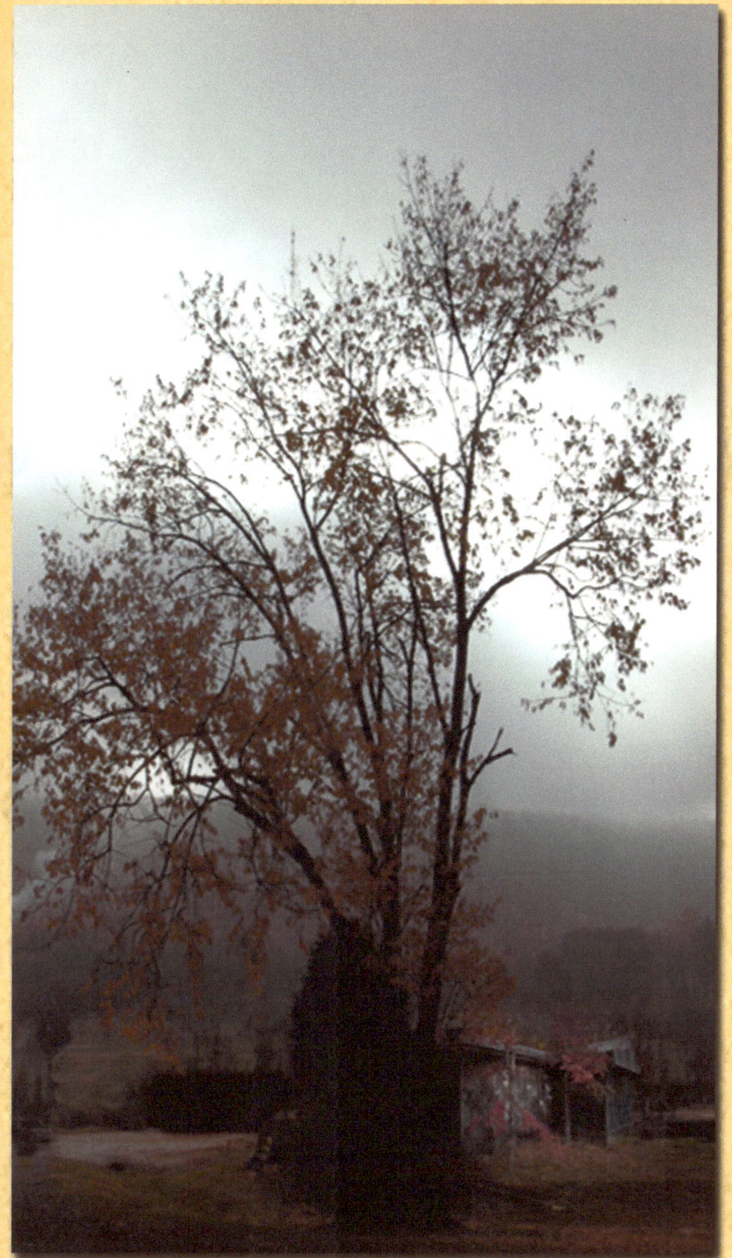

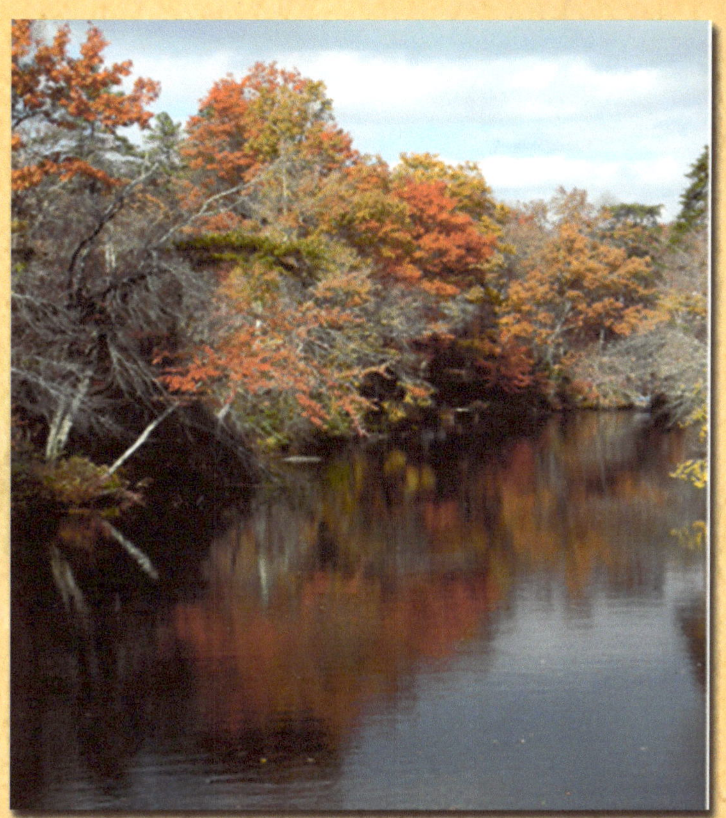

“Peace in the Valley”

In spite of, or perhaps because of the clouds and fog, the valley remains silent and serene, a security blanket for all living in the shadow of the mountain

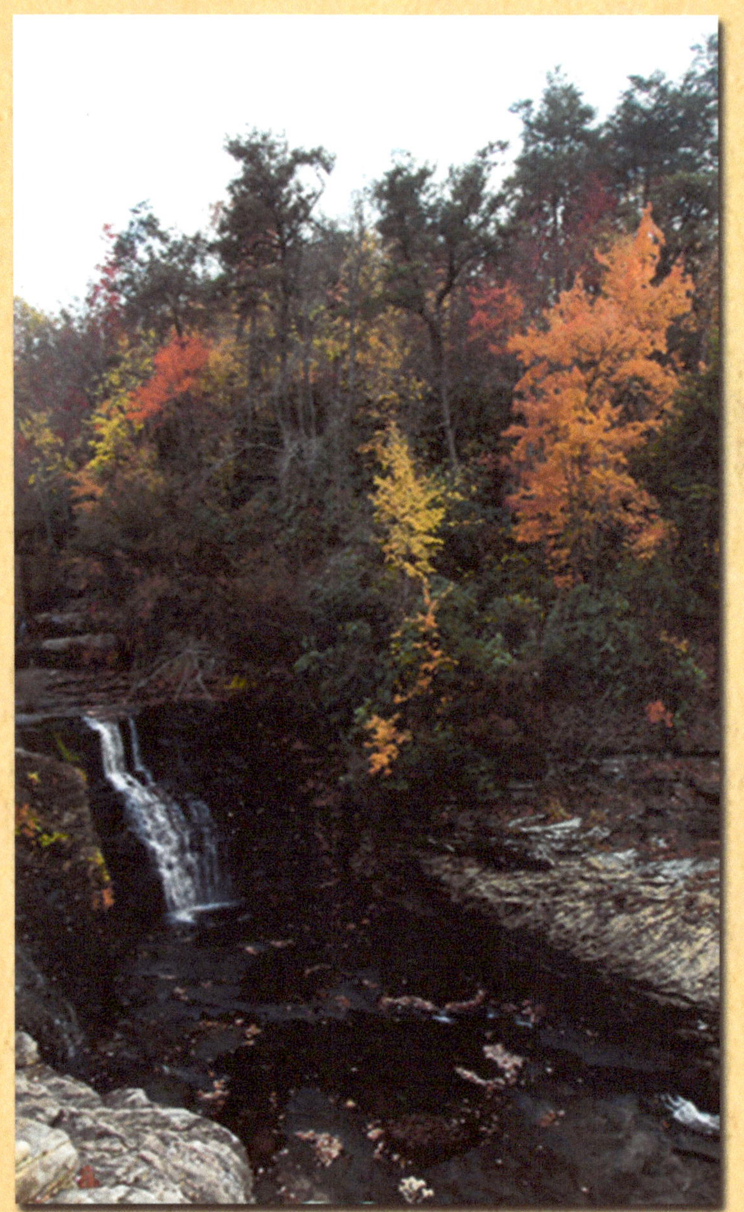

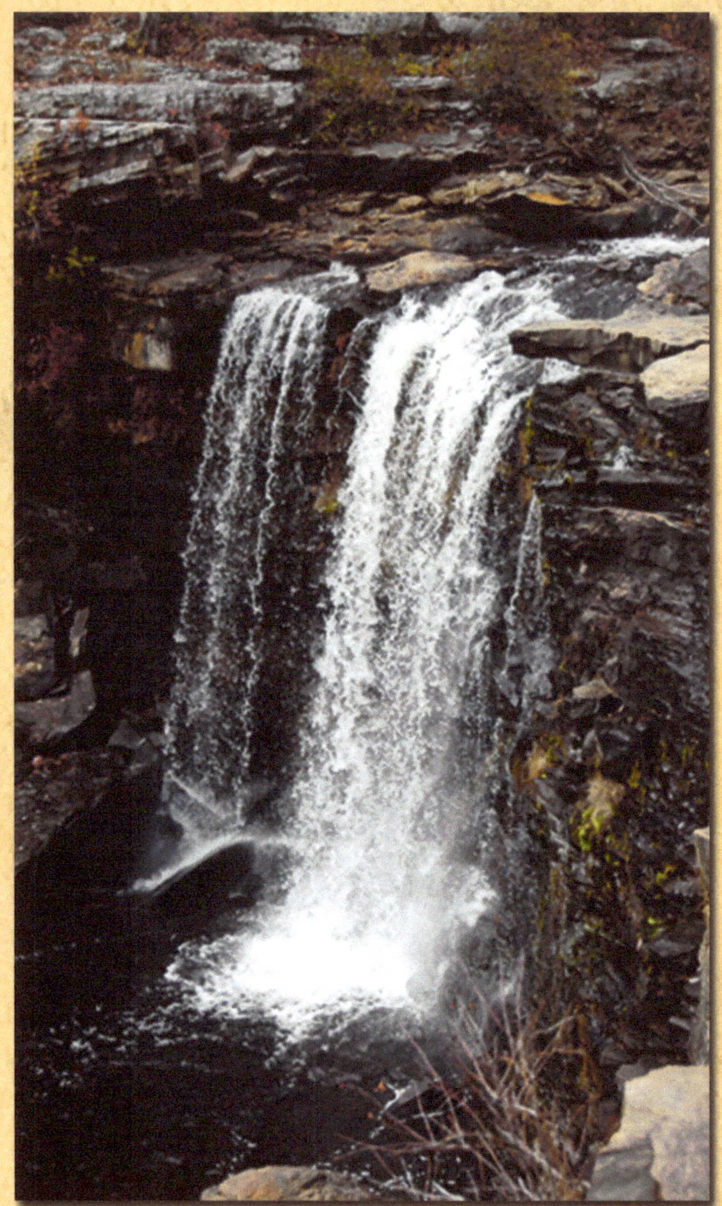

“Little River, Canyon and Falls”

Little River, a waterway that runs its entire course on top of a mountain.
The intensity of its meandering waters always
reflect a summer season of drought or rain.

Over millenniums, the force of its currents has carved intricate designs
on the bedrock inspiring poets and artists to capture them and bind them
to paper or canvas for posterity.

How many years have passed since nature decided this was the place
where all this life would happen?

Near the Trail of Tears, the falls witnessed some of the worst passages of
our history but they never stopped loving us and inspiring our soul while
nurturing our bodies with the precious water needed to sustain life.

Autumn moves on.
The water still Flows,
waiting for winter to cool its stone walls,
the last of the autumn leaves
hanging on to the rocks for as long as they can.

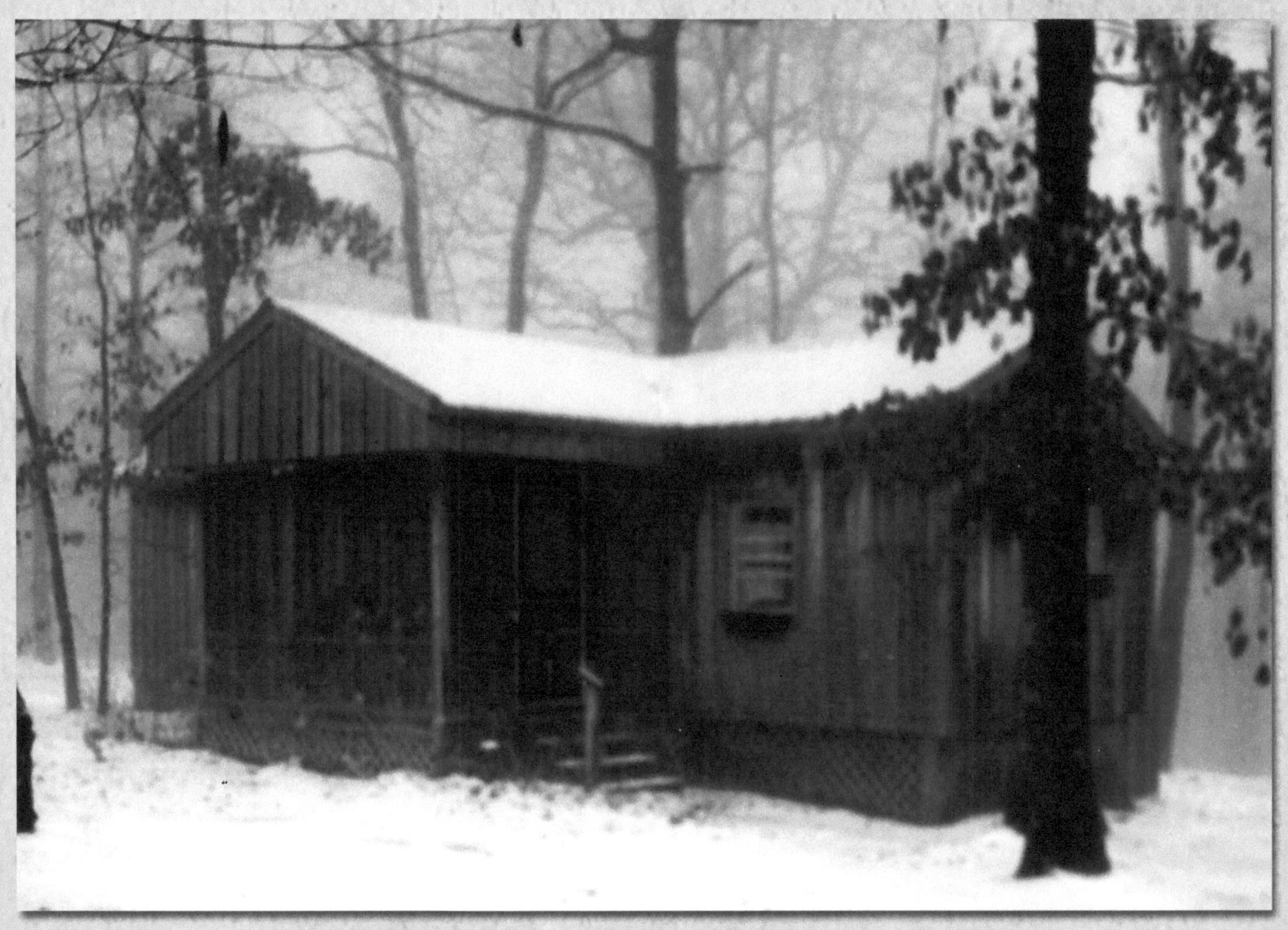

“Winter Peace at last”

The cabin is as lonely as it looks. No one lives there now, it has no one to talk to. The spirits of summers past have left.

Its seasoned walls are taking a rest, hoping for humans to visit to create fresh memories, and old ghosts to come back and haunt them.

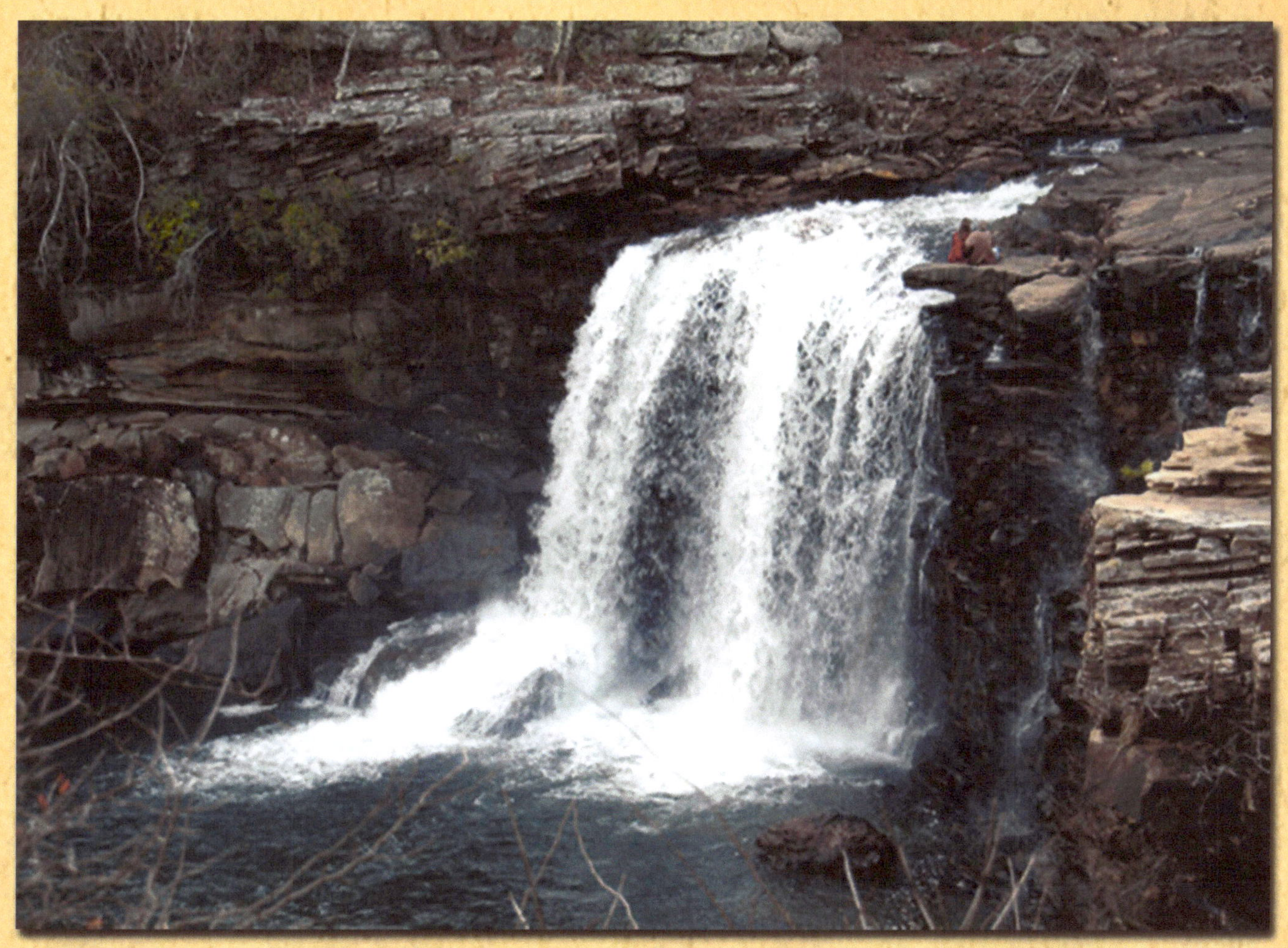

“Falling in Love”

To be with your lover at the top of the world.

Perched on the edge of the fall, you can dream of future happiness,
lulled by the peace and passion inspired by the roaring sounds of the water
and cooled by a soft winter breeze.

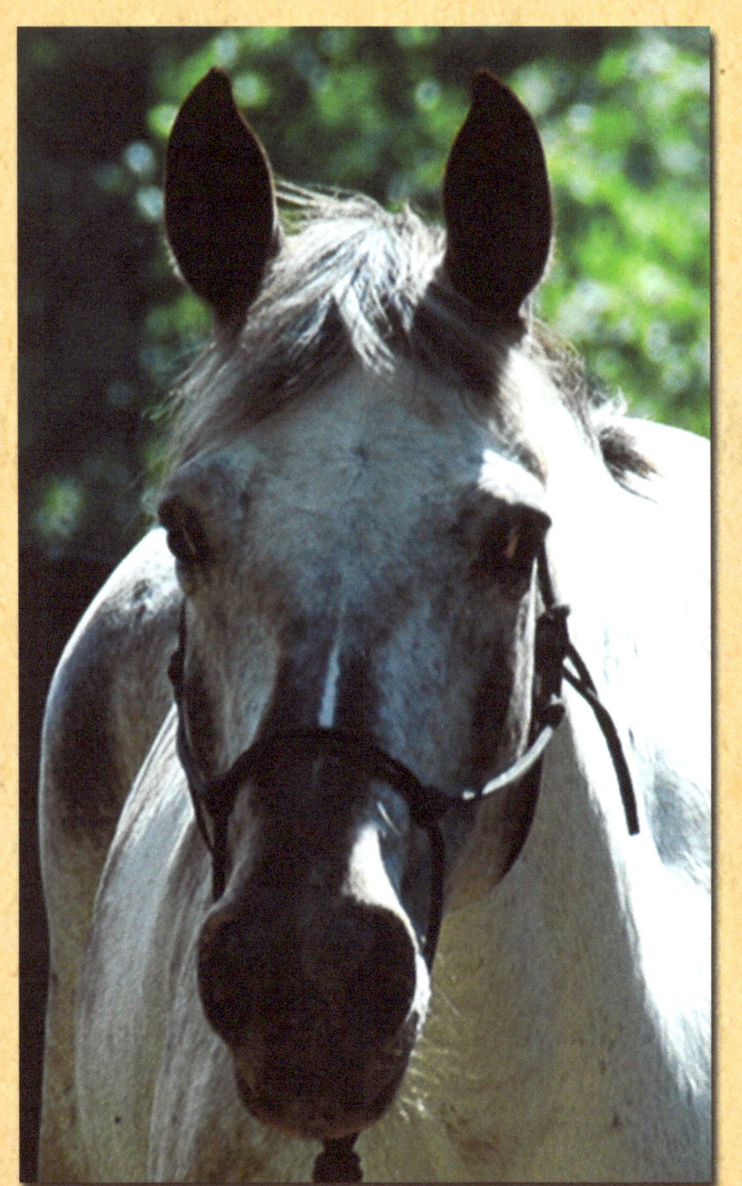

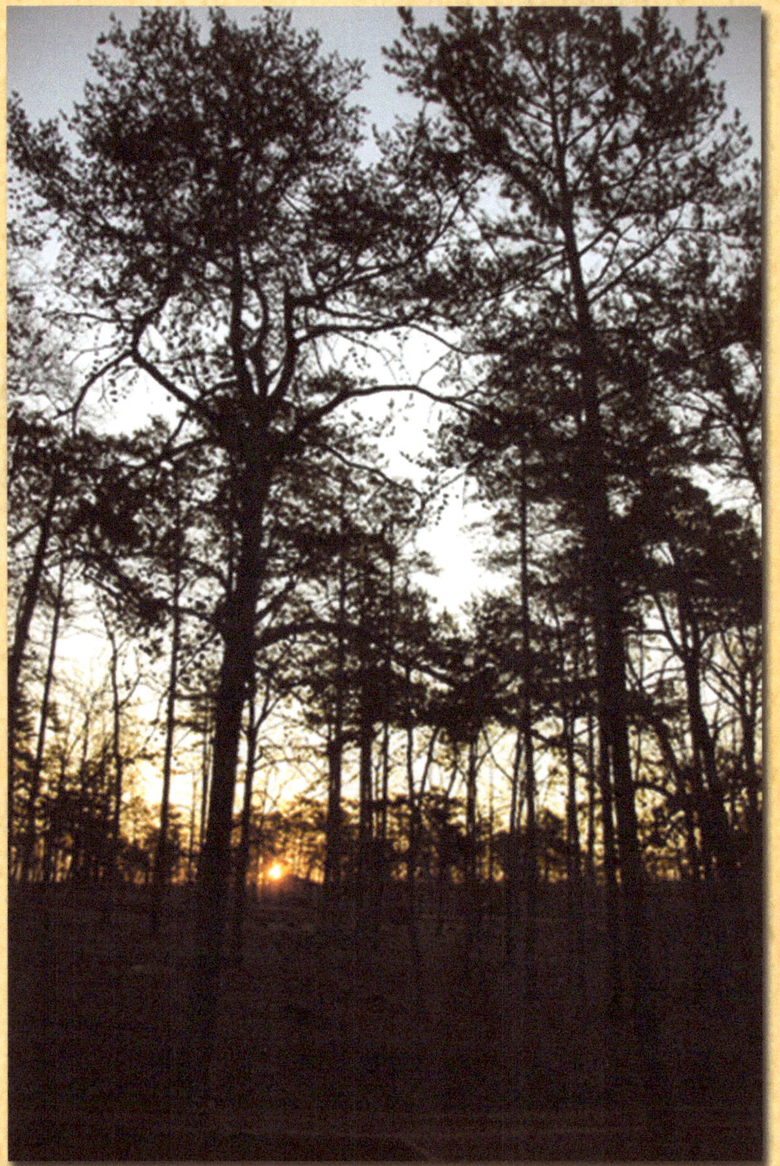

"The Symphony of Life's Seasons Goes on..."

The sun rises on the camp ground.
All is calm. Trees stand tall to meet their source of life.
Sounds of a horse's footsteps can be heard
from a nearby pasture. All is how it should be.

A new day awaits you and with it new worlds to explore.
Take care of where your steps lead you and
make sure that day is better after you have lived it
or maybe because you lived it.

If you are in harmony with nature, tomorrow will bring more sights
to behold, more water to fall in love with, and you will know as the
sun sets that this day was better because you were here.

Michèle Beaudin ©

www.ingramcontent.com/pod-product-compliance
Lightning Source LLC
LaVergne TN
LVHW070210110826
845147LV00002B/553

9780615324531